THE AGE OF THE NEW CAPITALISM

BY ROBERT R. CARKHUFF Ph.D.

FINANCIAL
CAPITAL

HUMAN AND
INFORMATION
CAPITAL

Cindy,
Best Regards,
Bob

Published by Human Resource Development Press, Inc.
22 Amherst Road
Amherst, Massachusetts 01002

ISBN No. 0-87425-070-6
First Printing June, 1988

Cover Design by John Alaimo
Word Processing by Susan Kotzin
Typesetting by The Magazine Group

DEDICATED

TO

JIM DRASGOW,

Mentor and friend,
who taught me the first law of thinking:
"Don't lose progress time!"
Which translated loosely means:
"Censor your bureaucratic conditioning
and get on with your productive thinking!"

FOREWORD

October 15, 1987, was "a shot heard round the world."
The tumbling market signaled the end of an era. It also signaled
what all executives now know—the beginning of the end of the
old capitalistic system as they have come to know it.

The old visions of capitalism have carried us as far as they
can. Executives are intensely aware that the economizing
benefits of restructuring and downsizing are drawing to an end.
They are searching desperately for new sources of growth.
Carkhuff's vision of *"The Age of the New Capitalism"* offers
the alternative of investing in people and ideas as the source of
potentially infinite productivity.

"The New Capitalism" is the first battle of the new American Revolution. It expands our vision of a new capital economy.
It enables us to invest in the prepotent sources of economic
growth—human and information capital. It allows us to emerge
as a new American nation—free of debt, free of deficits, free of
vulnerabilities and contingencies of the old capitalism.

The first American Revolution was a War of Independence.
It was fought to free the colonies of the pernicious and coercive
burdens imposed upon it by the exclusive mentality of the
mother country.

The new American Revolution is a War of Interdependence. It is being fought to free American citizenry of the
pernicious and coercive burdens of the exclusive mentality of
the old capitalistic way of thinking.

The central theme of the old capitalism is: *"It takes money
to make money!"* Based upon this theme, America has built
awesome industrial machinery capable of producing a seemingly
endless array of goods and services. In the process, it has seen
its people as extensions of that great machinery—whether on the
assembly line or in the executive suite. They have performed

"all that money has asked of them" and they have come up "empty"—devoid of new ideas, deficit in new sources of growth, dissatisfied with the levels of remuneration on their own terms. In short, they have concluded: *"We can't get there from here anymore—we simply can't make money by investing money!"*

The central theme of *"The New Capitalism"* is: *"It takes people to make money!"* People create the ideas that are transformed into the operational information upon which products and services are based. In short, human and information capital are the productive ingredients in the new economic equation. To support this conclusion, Carkhuff provides an economic data base that indicates that *human and information capital now account for 85 percent of economic productivity growth.*

What is needed is a technology to produce these potentially invaluable ingredients. Carkhuff has that—the first systematic thinking skills technologies. He has the thinking technologies that are the sources of human and information capital development. Indeed, his vision of *"The New Capitalism"* is based upon these sources.

He applies these thinking technologies to transform business and industry into *"productive thinking environments"* by empowering all personnel—at levels of all areas—to think productively. He secures the human resource inputs by imbedding in the thinking environments *"thinking centers"* that develop producers rather than consumers of information. He extends the results outputs into *"thinking markets"* in which sustaining relationships are based upon mutual productivity and profitability.

In this regard, it would be more proper to interpret the central theme of *"The New Capitalism"* as follows: *"It takes people to create wealth!"* For Carkhuff, wealth may be measured in terms of human and information capital byproducts as well as products and services. Indeed, Carkhuff suggests, thinking people and operational ideas may become more valuable than the very goods and services that they generate!

"The New Capitalism" is really an extension of the continuing American Revolution. Just as the Constitution created the nation and shared its power with its citizens politically, so will *"The New Capitalism"* create and extend the concept of wealth and its distribution to all contributors. Just as the Bill of Rights and Civil Rights freed American citizens physically and emotionally to make their contributions, so will *"The New Capitalism"* free them intellectually and interpersonally to actualize their contributions. Viewing the human mind as the rarest of all materials, *"The New Capitalism"* enables each person to become the source of new and heretofore untold wealth.

To be sure, Carkhuff's vision of *"The New Capitalism"* is accompanied by a new Bill of Rights:

- The rights of all citizens to contribute their creative ideas to the new economy.
- The rights of all citizens to process information and make decisions for productive economic purposes.
- The rights of all citizens to think themselves out of their jobs, trusting that new roles and challenges will be available to them.

There is also a new Bill of Rights for corporations:

- The right to capitalize upon thinking as the source of economic value.
- The right to benefit from new information breakthroughs by employees.
- The right to trust that investments in human and information capital will be dedicated to economic benefits.

Like the War of Independence, then, the new American Revolution will begin with the inspiration, commitment, and creative thinking of a few executives who will transform the vision into a mission. Soon the armies of thinkers from the homes and communities, schools and industries, governments and marketplaces, will provide the motivation, perspiration, and above all, productive thinking to accomplish the mission.

Make no mistake about it! *"The New Capitalism"* is a new American Revolution! It requires a Declaration of Interdependence: that every person is interdependent with every other person (production and delivery personnel along with executives and managers); that every organization is interdependent with every other organization (home, school, and business); that every community is interdependent with every other community (producers and consumers alike in the commerce of towns, cities, regions, states, and nations).

We are at war to free ourselves of the restrictive burdens of the old capitalism. Our weapons are our thinking skills. Our destiny is in our minds!

Jack Kelly
Retired Director
Information Systems
IBM

ROBERT R. CARKHUFF, PH.D.

- One of the most-cited social scientists of our time and author of three of the most-referenced books over the last two decades.

- Chairman and C.E.O. of Human Technology, Inc., one of the fastest-growing corporations in the U.S.A.

- A visionary of the New Capitalism based upon the new capital ingredients—human and information capital.

PREFACE

I have written this book for executives, decision makers, and opinion leaders who are beginning to realize that the string has run out on our ideas of capitalism. Insider trading and corporate raiding notwithstanding, financial capital is no longer the dominant ingredient in economic productivity growth. In its place are the two emerging ingredients: human capital, or people who think, and information capital, or operational information that can be translated into products and services. Together, in a synergistic relationship, where each grows as the other grows, these new capital ingredients define human processing, the prepotent factor in economic growth. The roles that these new capital ingredients play in creating a new capitalism will be the thesis of this book.

In writing this book, I have three objectives:

1. To introduce a unifying thinking theory of value that integrates internal and external human dynamics;
2. To introduce a new theory of capitalism in economics;
3. To introduce a new theory of thinking in psychology.

I sincerely hope that this work can reach into the minds and souls of a generation of "old capitalists" and expand their vision of the possible. I dedicate it to the next generation of "new capitalists" as a vision of the probable so that it may guide them in advancing our great civilization and, in the process, in discovering and fulfilling their own humanity. In the words of the old-timer to whom I first explained the theory on a flight to Canada, "If it's not too late for me, then it's not too early for others."

McLean, Virginia
June 1988

Robert R. Carkhuff, Ph.D.

ACKNOWLEDGMENTS

In preparing this book, I owe a special debt of gratitude to the following people who helped me enter the Age of the New Capitalism:

- The old capitalist who helped me articulate my ideas on the plane to Edmonton.
- The economists who provided a state-of-the-art data base for the prepotency of human and information capital: Anthony Carnavale, Edward Denison, C. Jackson Grayson, and John Kendrick.
- My colleague and teacher Bernard G. Berenson, who, more than anyone else, has helped me to put these ideas into perspective and to understand their implications for a unified science of human behavior.
- My wife Bernice, who has been a continuing source of inspiration and editorial feedback.
- My colleagues at Human Technology, Inc., who have stimulated and supported my work: John Cannon, Alex Douds, Sharon Fisher, Richard Pierce, Ray Vitalo, Don Benoit.
- Jim Barnet, who always has the eyes and ears of the ultimate consumer.
- Rick Bellingham, who helped me to communicate my ideas commercially.
- Dave Burleigh, who helped me position my ideas in relation to the marketplace.
- Jim Drasgow, who validated my perspectives when they counted most.
- Jack Kelly, who kept me in contact with the realities of business.

Without each and every one of these contributors, this work would never have been completed in its current form.

R.R.C.

TABLE OF CONTENTS

PROLOGUE:
ENTERING THE AGE OF
THE NEW CAPITALISM

CRITICAL PHASES OF HUMAN EVOLUTION

FIRST SIGNS OF LIFE — HOMONID

FOOD GATHERING — HOMO-SAPIENS

TOOL-MAKING

AGRARIAN

INDUSTRIAL

ELECTRONIC

INFORMATION

3.5 BILLION — 14 MILLION — 300,000 — 10,000 — 200 — 20 — NOW

I stretched across the empty seat to get my last look at Washington. As the plane ascended, the darkness washed out man's blinking lights. And I was alone with my thoughts.

They used to call Washington a capital city—meaning most important. As with Rome, all roads led to D.C. But all that is changing now. It seems as if people around the world don't look to D.C. like they used to. Maybe that's because D.C. never listened to them. Washington is a place where everybody talks and no one listens.

As we left Washington in darkness, I wrestled with the questions of another kind of darkness.

- Is the American century really over?
- Will consumer excesses and producer deficiencies bring us to our economic knees?
- Are we destined to pursue the "anthill" group mentalities of totalitarian systems that have imported our capitalism but not the individual freedom that gave it birth?

As we followed the eastern seaboard north, I wondered whether someone would write a verse to note our decline as Kipling had done in Britain's time:

"Far-called our navies melt away; on dune and headland sinks the fire."

A BACKWARD LOOK

As we descended upon New York, the city reminded me more of a big jar than a big apple, a jar in which we used to keep captured lightening bugs, all packed up so that one bug could not see the other's light, let alone its own reflection. In New York the empty seat next to me was taken. The passenger was an old-timer, straight and silver-mopped in appearance, alert and attentive in behavior. After exchanging greetings, we settled in for the flight to Toronto en route to Edmonton. The old-timer commented upon the city as we rose above it:

"There she is—once the city of need, now the city of greed!"

"Sounds like you're pretty cynical about the system," I said, trying to respond to his experience.

"Well, the system wasn't set up just to release a few greedy people to exploit the rest," he countered.

"That city was once America's answer to change," I offered.

The old-timer turned in his seat and attended to me vigilantly.

"By transforming lower-class immigrants and migrants into middle-class citizens, the city fostered a variety and richness of ideas to cope with the changing requirements of our environment," I continued.

"So social mobility is the response to change!"

"My friend, Bernie Berenson, says that God's secret is that the universe is inherently unstable," I responded.

"Then I guess man's secret is to attack the instability by creating variability," the old-timer concluded.

INSTABILITY AND VARIABILITY

On the flight to Toronto, I introduced myself and my professions—social scientist, educator, businessman, and citizen. The old-timer reciprocated in kind.

"Just think of me as an old capitalist. I remember when capitalism was good for everyone it touched."

"But not anymore?" I asked.

"Well, it seems like they're trying to drain the last few drops out of the old way of doing things..." The old capitalist drifted off.

"Instead of discovering the new ways," I reflected, attempting to be responsive.

"I don't really know what these new ways might be, but as an old capitalist I'm eager to learn."

Learning was to be a theme that he repeated many times over on the trip—and always related to capitalism. For this old capitalist, it seemed as if learning about changing conditions and ingredients was part and parcel of being a capitalist.

THE OLD CAPITALIST

I soon discovered that the old capitalist had grown up as a farmer on the great plains of Canada and was returning for the first time in forty years. In the interim, he had been a machinery businessman in Edmonton, a CEO of an electronics firm, a member of the stock exchange in Toronto, and now an investor in New York City.

"How exciting it is to have lived in all of these different ages!" the social scientist in me asserted.

"How's that?" he asked politely.

"To have begun in agrarian times, yet to have lived fully in the industrial, electronic and information eras!" I elaborated.

"It's true, I've lived the capitalist dream over several lifetimes."

"That's exciting?"

"Well, it's exciting and unnerving, too. It's exciting when we understand what we're doing. But it's unnerving when we don't."

"How's that?" I asked.

"Well, it used to be that we could figure out business enterprises and make our predictions. But I'll be danged if any of us knows what we're doing. We just can't predict the success of a business enterprise anymore. Things have changed too much."

THE HUMAN EXPERIENCE

"What are the main changes that you experience?" I asked.

"The people. People and information. The people know a lot more; they're a lot more skilled. They know how to use information. How to educate themselves with it. How to generate it. How to disseminate it."

"Then how is it that you can't predict economic success anymore?" I asked.

"If I knew the answer to that, I'd be many times over the success I've already been."

"Maybe you've already answered the question—people and information. Human and information resources are the new capital ingredients in economic success."

THE NEW CAPITAL INGREDIENTS

I. INTRODUCTION

1. INTRODUCTION

1. The Age of the Old Capitalism

STRATEGIES

MISSION

RESOURCES

PRODUCTION

MARKETING

DISTRIBUTION

PRODUCTS AND SERVICES

MARKETPLACE

REINVEST

The flight to Toronto was smooth in the air while sometimes rocky in conversation.

"I get a perspective in the open sky that I don't have in the walled-in city," the old capitalist volunteered.

"It's like flying across the ages. You get a chance to experience the feeling and meaning of life instead of just doing," I interpreted.

"Now you take Toronto down there. She's a sparkling city. **Toronto** *is the Huron Indian word for 'meeting place.' This used to be the meeting place for the overland route between Lake Ontario and Lake Huron."*

"That's exactly what commerce is, a meeting place. All relations between peoples begin with commerce between producer and consumer."

"That's what makes a great city. A great corporation. A great people."

"Commerce for mutual benefit—that's the basis for the New Capitalism."

"The New Capitalism?" the old capitalist queried.

THE OLD AND THE NEW

"The New Capitalism means that there are new capital ingredients," I responded.

"I always thought of capital in financial terms," said the old capitalist.

"All that capital really means is 'most important.' "

"So there can be many forms of capital, then, depending upon what's most important."

"Exactly. Now in the age of information, human and information capital are most important."

"Do we know this for sure?"

"Human and information capital account for 85 percent of economic productivity growth."

"You mean that only leaves 15 percent for financial capital?"

"Right. Financial capital is necessary but not sufficient for economic growth."

"I remember when land defined a person's wealth," the old capitalist mused.

"And so, someday, if we both live long enough, we will remember when finances determined a person's wealth."

THE MEANING OF CAPITAL

"I pretty much understand the capitalist system," the old
capitalist said. *"Basically, we invest capital to make capital
from marketing our products and services."*
"So what is capital?" I asked.
*"Well, we used to think about capital in terms of every-
thing that money would buy: labor, materials, equipment.
These were the things that we invested in our business."*
"And what is the purpose of capitalism?"
*"Why, to make money. To accumulate capital that we rein-
vest in the business. Capitalism is a cycle: we invest money
to make money."*
"Suppose I said, 'You can't get there from here'?"
"I wouldn't know what you meant," the old capitalist
answered.
*"You can no longer make money by simply investing
money!"*

A QUESTION OF CAPITALISM

We began with a discussion of capitalism in a free market. We agreed that many producers converge upon the marketplace to compete with their goods and services. Assuming an economy of scarcity, then, the market is governed by the laws of supply and demand: those producers who offer the highest-quality products at the lowest prices make the most sales.

"What are the producer benefits, then?" I asked.

"Why, to make a profit, usually by a combination of production efficiency and sales volume, sometimes with a combination of innovation and market niche."

"So producer profitability is the capitalistic ethic," I continued.

"Yes, we assume that the consumers will get the most value for the price by this system," the old capitalist replied.

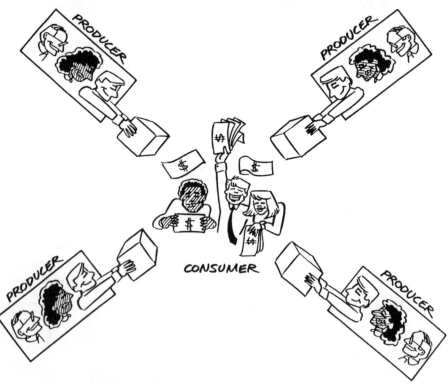

PROFITABILITY—THE CAPITALIST ETHIC

We extended our discussion to the corporate mission. In defining the corporate mission, the executives usually target specific consumer populations to whom the corporation will market products and services. The corporation's goals are to be profitable in the business of selling and delivering the products and services.

"So the consumer is the target but the producer is the real beneficiary," the old capitalist interpreted. *"The producer deals with consumers as a means of achieving the producer's goals."*

"It's interesting that the producer does not have the same benefit goals for consumers as it does for itself," I countered.

"The corporation is in it for its own benefits," he said. *"So profitability, then, is the basic value of capitalism."*

CONSUMER TARGETS

· CONSUMERS

PRODUCER GOALS

· PROFITIBILITY

CAPITALISM BEGINS WITH THE CORPORATE MISSION

We then considered the corporate strategies employed to achieve the mission. Although today most mature corporations are market driven, historically many companies were driven by product resources such as energy or production such as particular product lines. In any event, together these strategies dictate the organizational design and operations that enable us to accomplish the mission.

"Originally, we just produced the products and then figured out how to market them," said the old capitalist. *"Today we research consumer needs and try to meet them with our goods and services."*

"So your strategies are sources of action for accomplishing your mission," I said.

"Yes, they become the sources of our organization and its operations."

CAPITALISM IS IMPLEMENTED BY CORPORATE STRATEGIES

For example, in the capitalistic system our strategic components or processing operations are derived from our strategies. The different levels of the processing operations have responsibilities for different outputs. Ultimately, the resource inputs are transformed into results outputs by processing.

"Even if it's only one entrepreneur, the person needs to think things through at all of these levels in all of these areas," the old capitalist inserted.

"So the heart of the capitalistic system is the processing operations that transform resource inputs into results outputs."

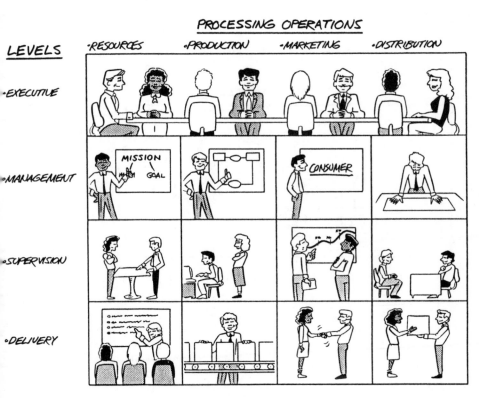

CAPITAL RESOURCES ARE PROCESSED

In this context, then, the basic fuel of capitalism is capital as we have traditionally defined it.

"We've always defined capital resources in terms of the resources that money could buy," the old capitalist chimed in. *"We saw our finances as the source of all the other resources we needed to invest in order to accomplish our mission: labor, information, materials, equipment, and the like."*

"Financial resources were viewed as the primary source of all other resources," I responded.

CAPITAL RESOURCES ARE INVESTED

In turn, the results of the processing are the products and services that are offered for sale in the marketplace.

"The products and services are a means to an end in the capitalistic system," the old capitalist noted. *"We produced our products to impact our markets."*

"The products and services are the producer's offerings in the marketplace."

"They allow us to exchange with the consumer in the marketplace."

"And accomplish your profitability mission."

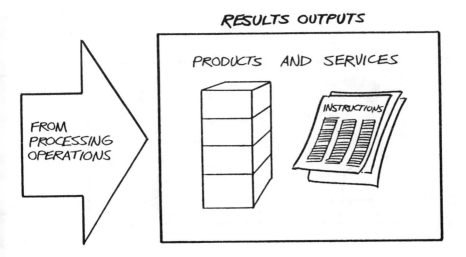

CAPITAL PRODUCTS ARE PRODUCED

The goal of the production of products and the delivery of services, then, is to sell them in the marketplace.

"It's in the marketplace that the products and services are transformed into real capital," the old capitalist indicated. *"Our products weren't worth anything if we couldn't sell them."*

"So the economic value of the products and services was determined by how well you anticipated and satisfied consumer needs," I responded.

"Yes, consumer sales are the means to financial capital."

"The raison d'etat *of capitalism!"* I exclaimed.

**CAPITAL PRODUCTS ARE SOLD
IN THE MARKETPLACE**

The capitalistic system is culminated by transforming the products and services into capital, which is dispersed to owners and shareholders or reinvested in capital resource inputs.

"From money to money is the thesis of capitalism as we have practiced it," the old capitalist concluded. *"I raise money to invest. I make money to reinvest."*

"So the capitalistic system is recycled over and over," I said. *"Businesses make the money that enables them to survive and grow."*

"The problem is that we can't project or predict economic growth in this way anymore."

"You can't get there from here!" I remarked.

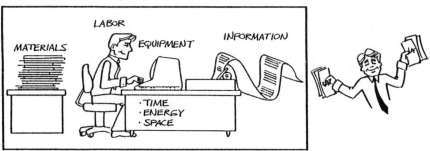

CAPITAL IS ACCUMULATED AND REINVESTED

"The laws of supply and demand do not operate in the same way in an economy of abundance as in an economy of scarcity," I reflected. *"An economy of abundance means that the consumer can pick or choose from producers—even more, can demand products and services that do not now exist."*

"And these consumer demands become producer requirements?" queried the old capitalist.

"Exactly!" I answered. *"The issue confronting the old capitalism is this: How do you cooperate with the consumer in order to compete in the market?"*

"No more cheap, off-the-shelf products, huh?" the old capitalist asked.

"Not even cheap, customized products."

"Only cheap, tailored products?" he questioned again.

"Now you've got the idea. The New Capitalism must be consumer driven."

"So the producer profitability ethic no longer dominates."

"It can be met only if the consumer profitability ethic is also met."

"I guess that's what they mean by interdependency."

"Exactly. Interdependency is the keynote of the New Capitalism."

"But how is it accomplished?" the old capitalist asked.

"That is the challenge of the New Capitalism."

THE CHALLENGE OF THE NEW CAPITALISM

The old capitalist summarized his vision of the old capitalistic system:

> *"The old capitalistic system brings to mind the old carts we used when I first was in farming. Basically, we were pulled by finances and pushed by products. We pretty much took our goods to market without knowing what to expect. We assumed the labor part of human resources and read the Farmer's Almanac for information. Come to think of it, by putting the horse before the cart we may have slowed ourselves down in the Information Age."*

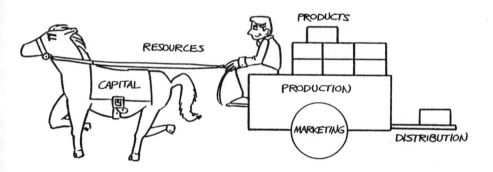

THE OLD CAPITAL VEHICLE

II. THE NEW CAPITAL SYSTEMS

2. The Performance Source of Productivity

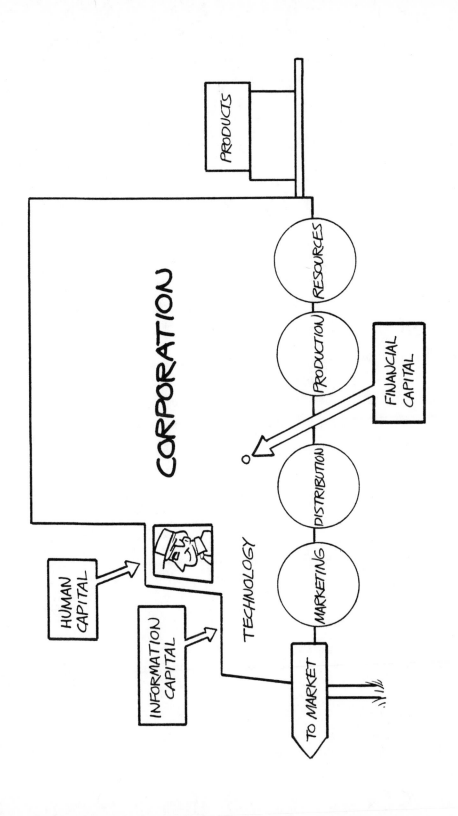

The plane labored in the face of an Alberta Clipper on the way to Edmonton. It gave us plenty of time to explore the New Capitalism.

"You know, returning to Edmonton is like returning to the past," the old capitalist contemplated.

"We're only bound to the past if we think like the past," I added.

"So if we free ourselves of our old ways of thinking, we can learn the new ways," he reflected.

"The old ways didn't involve thinking," I answered. *"We were simply conditioned to react reflexively to specific situations."*

"And now, you're saying, we need to learn how to think things through."

"That's right!" I exclaimed. *"Thinking is really the source of the New Capitalism."*

"I'm interested in a whole new model of capitalism..."

"With a thinking person at the wheel!" I interjected.

IN SEARCH OF A NEW MODEL

"So the processing operations do not operate in vacuo," the old capitalist commented. *"They are performed by people."*
"Right. Human capital—people capable of thinking."
"So the people process information," he added.
"Information capital—operational information that can be acted upon," I explained.
"So people and information are the critical ingredients," the old capitalist continued to respond.
"Exactly. Human and information capital are the critical sources of performance."
"I think I've got it. Thinking is the source of performance and performance is the source of productivity," the old capitalist concluded. *"It's just like any business. First, I have to think about the best ways of doing things. Next, I have to get things organized to do them. Finally, I have to see how well we're doing them."*

THE PERFORMANCE SOURCES OF PRODUCTIVITY

I presented the relationship of human and information capital as the key idea in performance. Human and information capital relate synergistically. This means that each one contributes to the other's growth. Together, in this synergistic relationship, they define human processing as systematic thinking, which produces operational information.

"It sounds like people grow as they process information," the old capitalist commented.

"And the information grows as it is processed by people," I added.

THE PROCESSING SOURCE OF PERFORMANCE

To put human processing in the context of the processing operations is to insert thinking people and operational information within each of the cells of the operation.

"Thinking really has to take place at every level of the organization," the old capitalist said.

"And every person has to have the information appropriate to his or her processing tasks," I added.

"So every person has to receive and produce operational information."

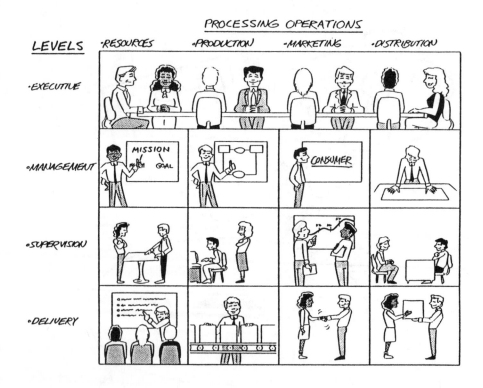

THE PROCESSING OPERATIONS

Relatedly, the sources of performance emphasize human processing by the individual, by units or groups of individuals, and by the entire organization. The sources of performance are the human and information capital processing that go on within these categories.

"What it all adds up to is how productively people think— single individuals, units or groups, or entire organizations of people," the old capitalist concluded.

"People are the source of performance."

SOURCES OF PERFORMANCE

∘ INDIVIDUAL PERFORMANCE   ∘ UNIT PRODUCTION   ∘ ORGANIZATION PRODUCTIVITY

THE SOURCES OF PERFORMANCE

"For example," I continued, *"the individual performance system emphasizes human processing to improve the productivity of responses performed at individual stations."* The old capitalist traced the individual performance system: *"We invest human and information capital along with financial capital. We process by thinking productively. We perform responses increasingly more effectively and efficiently."*
"People perform the responses that produce the products and services," I added.

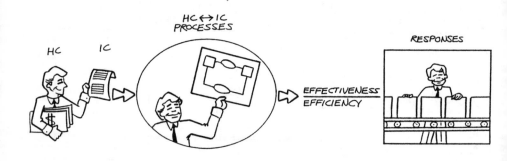

THE INDIVIDUAL PERFORMANCE SYSTEM

Within units thinking performers interact to add value to the parts they are producing and the communications to other units they are delivering.

The old capitalist overviewed the unit production system:

"Our capital inputs are processed by many performers to improve the productivity of the parts and communicate to adjacent units."

"Groups of people produce the parts that ultimately make up the products and services," I added.

THE UNIT PRODUCTION SYSTEM

Finally, we viewed the entire organizational productivity system dedicated to the production of products and services.

The old capitalist traced the organizational productivity system:

> *"Managers and employees process capital inputs together to improve the quantity and quality—while reducing the costs—of products and services."*
>
> *"That's right. Everybody gets together to produce the products and services."*

THE ORGANIZATIONAL PRODUCTIVITY SYSTEM

The old capitalist responded to my prodding to put the picture of productive processing operations together:

"Basically, the processing operations change the capital inputs into capital outputs. The source of their productivity is performance—individual, unit, and organizational."

"And the source of performance is thinking," I added.

LEVELS:	RESOURCES			PRODUCTION			MARKETING			DISTRIBUTION		
	IND. PERF	UNIT PROD	ORG PROD	IND PERF	UNIT PROD	ORG PROD	IND PERF	UNIT PROD	ORG PROD	IND PERF	UNIT PROD	ORG PROD
EXECUTIVE												
MANAGEMENT												
SUPERVISION												
DELIVERY												

PRODUCTIVE PROCESSING OPERATIONS

"So performance is the source of productivity," the old capitalist concluded.

"And thinking is the source of performance," I repeated.

"Yes, the real power of performance lies in the relationship between thinking people and operational information."

"The real source of performance is ideas," I commented. The old capitalist nodded his head. *"I feel more powerful just understanding how these things work."*

"That's just the point," I continued. *"Teaching thinking empowers people to contribute their performance to overall productivity."*

"Now, I'm really excited," the old capitalist remarked. *"I've got to learn about the thinking sources of performance."*

THE REAL POWER OF PERFORMANCE

The old capitalist summarized the performance source of productivity:

"The goal of improving performance is to create a productive environment. A productive environment is one in which people think productively, as individuals at their work stations, as groups within their working units, as organizations or corporations. Where people think and work together in the common cause of a mission. The question is, how do you develop thinking people?"

CREATING THE PRODUCTIVE ENVIRONMENT

3. The Thinking Source of Performance

·RESOURCES
·PRODUCTION
·MARKETING
·DISTRIBUTION
MISSION
MISSION
GOAL
CONSUMER

"See those plains below?" the old capitalist asked, referring to the Canadian prairie below. *"An Englishman named William Francis Butler called it the Great Lone Land: 'This ocean has no past—time has been nought to it; and men have come and gone, leaving behind them no track, no vestige of their presence,' "* he quoted.

"Civilizations come and go but few leave their mark," I responded.

"Then how does one civilization leave its mark while another leaves no vestige?" he asked.

"By learning and thinking. Learning to adjust to changing environmental conditions. Thinking to create your own changing conditions."

"Learning enables us to adapt," the old capitalist responded.

"We increase our responses to cover all situations."

"And thinking enables us to create."

"We create new responses and new situations!"

"Now as we enter the Information Age, we need to learn both the adaptive and the creative responses."

"If we are to leave our track—"

"And lead to a Great Full Land!"

THINKING AND THE ADVANCEMENT OF CIVILIZATION

"So human and information capital are the critical ingredients of economic growth," the old capitalist continued.
"People and ideas!" I exclaimed.
"Human capital is defined by thinking people. And information capital is defined by the ideas they produce."
"But the ideas must be in an operational form capable of being translated into goods and services in the marketplace."
"And these people and ideas impact upon each other . . ."
"Like what's going on between us right now!"
"Our ideas stimulate each other's growth."
"That's exactly what human capital is—the power to think."
"So what we really need is information capital for producing human and information capital."
"A technology of thinking!" I exclaimed.

NEW CAPITAL-BASED ECONOMIC GROWTH

"So how do people learn thinking?" the old capitalist asked.

"There are really three sources of human processing: thinking, relating, planning," I offered.

The old capitalist leaned forward. *"Let me see if I understand,"* he remarked. *"First, we think about things by ourselves. Then we relate to share our ideas and develop new ideas. Finally, we plan to implement the ideas."*

"Exactly!" I responded. *"Thinking independently. Relating interpersonally. Planning organizationally."*

"So if we think, relate, and plan in this way, we'll increase our performance."

"Absolutely. And do you know why?" I asked.

"Sure. Instead of just following orders, everybody becomes a source of ideas. Everybody becomes a source of value, a thinking source of performance," the old capitalist answered.

THE THINKING SOURCES OF PERFORMANCE

Again, I emphasized human processing as the key idea in performance. In human processing human and information capital relate synergistically. The trick is to see units of human processing interacting with each other to add value to each other.

"Let me see if I can say that another way," the old capitalist replied. *"The basic unit of human processing is an individual who thinks systematically. When individuals relate to other individuals, they process interpersonally. When a group of individuals focus upon planning organizational tasks, they process organizationally. Thinking! Relating! Planning!"*

THINKING   RELATING   PLANNING

THE THINKING SOURCES OF PERFORMANCE

Continuing in this vein, we put human processing in the context of the processing operations—to insert thinking within each unit of performance: individual, unit, and organizational performance.

"So thinking, relating, and planning have to take place within all units of performance," the old capitalist responded.

"And this has to occur at every level of the processing operations," I added.

PROCESSING COMPONENTS

·INDIVIDUAL
PERFORMANCE

·UNIT
PRODUCTION

·ORGANIZATION
PRODUCTIVITY

THE SOURCES OF PERFORMANCE

I introduced the sources of thinking. Individual processing emphasizes the individual thinking systematically and independently. Interpersonal processing involves two or more individuals thinking systematically and interpersonally. Organizational functioning emphasizes groups of people planning systematically and interdependently to discharge organizational functions.

"To me, it's still thinking, relating, and planning," the old capitalist reacted.

"Thinking and relating add value. Planning ensures that we achieve that value," I emphasized.

SOURCES OF THINKING

THE SOURCES OF THINKING

Individual thinking transforms the raw data of human experience into operational information by processing systematically: exploring where we are; understanding where we want or need to be; acting to get there. Again, operational information is information capital that others can act upon.

"So individual thinking is a systematic way of producing useful information," the old capitalist concluded.

"Operational information means that the operations can be implemented and, ultimately, transformed into products and services."

INDIVIDUAL THINKING

It is helpful to look at the thinking system as a series of doors through which we must pass: exploring by analyzing our current experience; understanding by synthesizing our goals; acting by operationalizing our programs. Defining our goals in terms of our performance is the key that unlocks these doors or phases of thinking.

"So thinking is a process of systematically adding value," the old capitalist responded thoughtfully.

"That's right. First, we explore our current operations. Next, we understand our goals for productive operations. Finally, we act upon programs to achieve our productive goals."

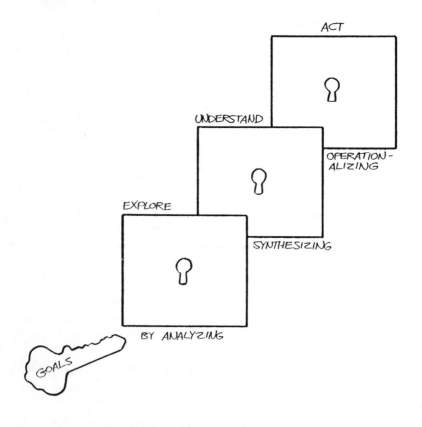

PHASES OF INDIVIDUAL THINKING

"For example," I continued, *"managers may analyze their current systems, synthesize productive systems, and operationalize productive programs to implement productive systems."*

"There really are systematic ways to think about improving performance, production, and productivity," the old capitalist commented.

"We call these skills productive thinking skills, or PTS," I interjected.

"They can help us to achieve any goals?" the old capitalist asked.

"Yes. Remember, the goals are the keys to our thinking systems."

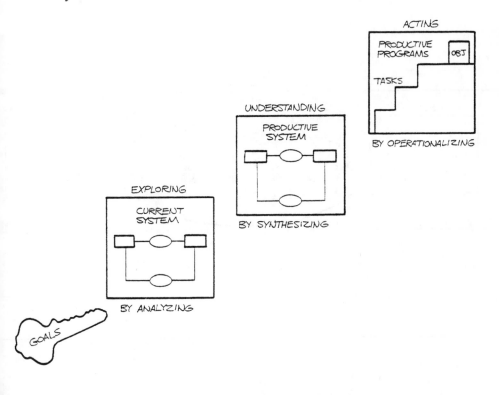

OPERATIONS OF INDIVIDUAL THINKING

I continued to explain that interpersonal processing is a way of adding still greater value to our original responses. In other words, two or more people get together to share their images of responses after thinking individually.

"Let me see if I can follow this illustration," the old capitalist responded. *"In this case, the individuals process the data independently into their own images of productive information. Next, they get together to share their images of the information. Finally, they process this new input interpersonally to create a whole new image of the information."*

I smiled and shook my head affirmatively. *"You got it! Each stage of processing adds value to information."*

INTERPERSONAL PROCESSING

One way to look at the phases of interpersonal processing is in terms of "get," "give," and "merge." First, we *get* the other's image of the information. Second, we *give* our own image of the information. Third, we negotiate to *merge* and even elevate images of the information.

"I like to say, 'We're going to do things your way, my way, or our way,'" the old capitalist commented.

"And if we process interpersonally, we may create totally new ways of doing things," I added.

"Maybe we can learn to go the 'high way.'"

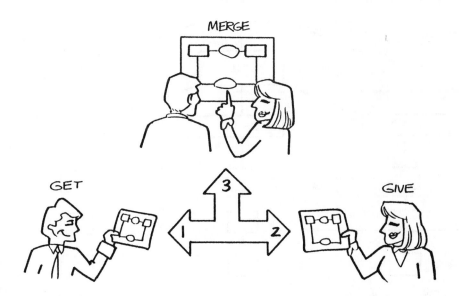

PHASES OF INTERPERSONAL PROCESSING

Organizational functioning is a way of ensuring "value added" benefits by planning. At most levels of functioning, it emphasizes planning: missions, strategies, systems, objectives, programs. Typically, we plan tasks that implement objectives, achieve goals, and accomplish missions.

"It seems to me," the old capitalist remarked, *"that each level guides the next level in planning. Each level enables the next level in execution."*

"Yes, these are the planning skills we are most familiar with," I remarked.

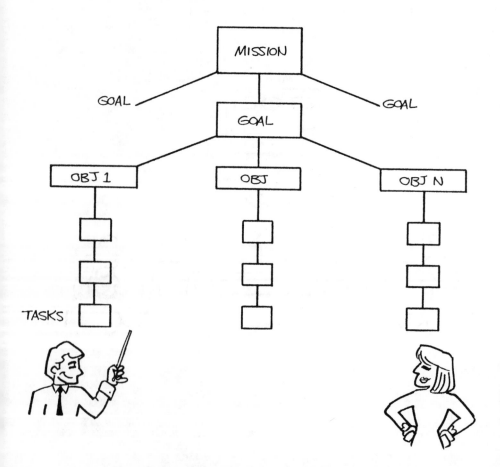

ORGANIZATIONAL FUNCTIONING

It may be helpful to view organizational functioning in terms of the phases of planning.

"I note how the output of each phase of planning becomes the information input of the next phase of planning," the old capitalist remarked.

"Exactly," I responded. *"This ensures that the value added in individual and interpersonal processing is translated into tangible benefits."*

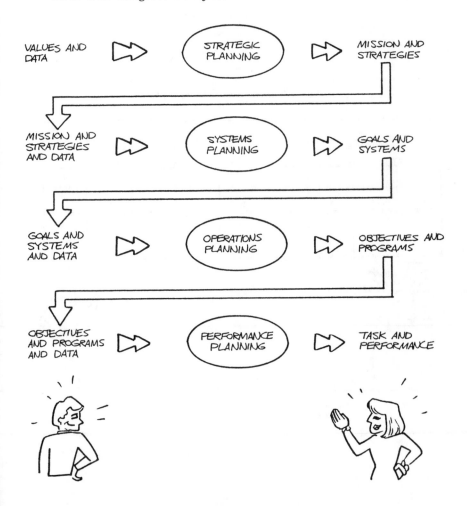

THE PHASES OF PLANNING

Now the old capitalist put the picture of the productive organization together:

"Basically, thinking, relating, and planning account for the performance of individuals, units, and organizations at every level of every processing operation. This enables the processing operations to transform capital inputs into capital outputs."

PROCESSING COMPONENTS

INDIVIDUAL PERFORMANCE			UNIT PRODUCTION			ORGANIZATION PRODUCTIVITY		
IND. THINK'G	INTERP. PROC'G	ORG. FUNCT'G	IND. THINK'G	INTERP. PROC'G	ORG. FUNCT'G	IND. THINK'G	INTERP. PROC'G	ORG. FUNCT'G

THE PRODUCTIVE ORGANIZATION

"So performance is the source of productivity and thinking is the source of performance," the old capitalist continued. *"Exactly. Thinking adds value exponentially." "Then thinking individually and interpersonally adds value, and planning organizationally ensures the achievement of that value." "The real power of thinking, however, lies in the ability to think systematically to achieve goals,"* I emphasized. The old capitalist thought a moment. *"So human capital is the source of ideas, but learning to think systematically empowers people to produce valuable information capital. I'm eager to learn how to think."*

THE REAL POWER OF THINKING

The old capitalist summarized the thinking source of performance:

> *"It seems to me the real goal of thinking is to create a productive thinking environment. It's not just a productive environment. It's a thinking environment dedicated to productive purposes. People are there to find a better way of doing things. To think themselves out of their jobs and to move on to the next level or area."*

PRODUCTIVE
THINKING
ENVIRONMENT

THE PRODUCTIVE THINKING ENVIRONMENT

4. The Educational Source of Thinking

"Somewhere down there on the plains is a little old school-house where it all started for me," the old capitalist said, beckoning to the brown blur below.

"Those little old schoolhouses are where it started for everyone," I added.

"Learning the basic skills and citizenship," the old capitalist contemplated.

"But what about learning to think and to capitalize?" I asked.

"Those are two areas that are left out of our curriculum."

"That's why the schools may soon be left out of the capitalist system."

"Either they can contribute to the economy or they will be left out of the economy."

"You're becoming committed to the thinking source of value," I reflected.

SCHOOLING AND THE NEW CAPITALISM

"Most educational programs teach memorizing rather than thinking," the old capitalist initiated.

"Yet 80 percent of human and information resource development is accounted for by education," I countered.

"What are the differences between education and training?" he asked.

"Typically, training is performance based, while education is processing based."

"So most of the programs calculated to improve performance are training programs."

"Yes, training programs work when you know the precise functions to be performed. For the most part, we simply condition people to perform these functions reflexively."

"What happens when the functions may require different responses under different conditions?" the old capitalist inquired.

"We simply train to increase the performer's repertoire of conditioned responses so that he or she can make fine discriminations of the conditions and, thus, select and apply the appropriate response," I answered.

"What happens when you don't know or the functions change?"

"You educate people with the generic processing skills and teach them how to transfer learnings."

"So you teach them how to process changing conditions," the old capitalist concluded thoughtfully.

THE EDUCATION SOURCES OF THINKING

We discussed further the functions of education and training—priming the capitalizing system. Priming emphasizes developing prime human and information capital to invest in the capitalizing system.

"So the real function of education is to develop human and information capital," the old capitalist reflected.

"That's right," I commented. *"We may think of resource components as being in the business of capital formation— human and information as well as financial."*

"Without priming, then, the system will not work."

PRIMING THE CAPITALIZING SYSTEM

In this context, we explored the instructional system. Human and information resource inputs are transformed into human and information capital by human and information resource development.

"Again, the human and information resources are developed synergistically in relation to each other," I said.

"This means that the human resources produce valuable information and, in turn, are impacted by information."

"It means they grow together," I commented.

"Like in a loving relationship!" the old capitalist added.

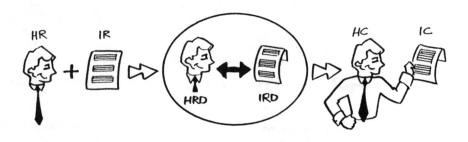

THE INSTRUCTIONAL SYSTEM

The instructional system serves to prime the processing operations. The operations must be analyzed at all levels in order to facilitate the processing: the strategic processes that accomplish missions; the management systems that accomplish goals; the supervisory programs that achieve objectives; and the delivery steps that perform tasks.

"Instructional design requires processing analysis," the old capitalist reflected.

"Instructional systems require the same processing as other systems," I added.

"So their goal is to transform their current operating systems into productive systems in order to help the processing operations do likewise."

PROCESSING OPERATIONS

PRIMING THE PROCESSING OPERATIONS

Specifically, the instructional system serves to prime the performance systems: individual performance, unit production, and organizational productivity.

"Instructional systems make these performance systems productive within the processing operations," the old capitalist responded.

"These performance systems have to be analyzed just as the processing operations within which they occur."

"That's what makes instruction useful and productive."

SOURCES OF PERFORMANCE

INDIVIDUAL PERFORMANCE	UNIT PRODUCTION	ORGANIZATION PRODUCTIVITY

PRIMING THE PRODUCTIVE PERFORMANCES

Instruction in processing skills is the source of improvement in performance and, ultimately, productivity growth.

"Education in processing skills is the most leveraged investment executives can make," I said.

"It makes sense! If thinking, relating, and planning are the productive ingredients of human and information capital, and human and information capital are the productive ingredients of productivity growth, then education in processing skills is the most leveraged source of economic growth," the old capitalist concluded.

SOURCES OF PROCESSING

INDIVIDUAL THINKING	INTERPERSONAL PROCESSING	ORGANIZATIONAL FUNCTIONING

EDUCATION IN PROCESSING SKILLS

"Of course, these generic processing skills require different forms of content at different levels of processing," I continued.

"It looks like the complexity of processing increases with the complexity of information inputs and outputs," the old capitalist commented.

AREAS OF PROCESSING

LEVELS		•INDIVIDUAL	•INTERPERSONAL	○ORGANIZATIONAL	
EXECUTIVE	VALUES AND DATA	CREATIVE THINKING	INCLUSIVE LEADERSHIP	POLICY MAKING	MISSION AND STRATEGIES
MANAGEMENT	MISSION AND STRATEGIES AND DATA	SYSTEMS THINKING	INTERPERSONAL MANAGEMENT	SYSTEMS PLANNING	GOALS AND SYSTEMS
SUPERVISION	GOALS AND SYSTEMS AND DATA	OPERATIONS THINKING	INTERPERSONAL FACILITATION	OPERATIONS PLANNING	OBJECTIVES AND PROGRAMS
DELIVERY	OBJECTIVES AND PROGRAMS AND DATA	TECHNICAL THINKING	INTERPERSONAL RELATING	TECHNICAL PERFORMANCE	TASKS AND STEPS

THE CORE THINKING SKILLS CONTENT

"This doesn't mean that we abandon training content, does it?" the old capitalist inquired.

"Absolutely not!" I exclaimed. *"Unique kinds of specialty content at all levels must interact with the core thinking content."*

The old capitalist looked at me for a moment. *"In other words, the personnel get a chance to think about the specialty content. Maybe they'll discover that it's not really unique."*

"That's just the point. By processing the content, the personnel establish its value and viability."

"Gee, I know corporations that spend hundreds of millions of dollars a year on thousands of independent courses that they probably could reduce to a handful of courses built around the core of thinking content."

"How about that!" I responded with a smile.

UNIQUE SPECIALTY SKILLS CONTENT

"Right now, by the time industry designs a new training program, the need has changed," the old capitalist said, stimulating me.

"By concentrating upon an educational core of processing skills," I said, *"we can now respond to that challenge."*

"The personnel are empowered to process or even generate their own training content in specialty functions."

"Thinking before training!" I exclaimed.

THE EDUCATIONAL CORE

"We used to say, 'You get what you train for.' Now we have to say, 'You get what you educate for'!"
"Yes," I responded. *"If you train for conditioned responses, that's what you'll get. If you educate for processing and transfer, that's what you'll get,"*
"But conditioning has a life!" the old capitalist reacted.
"Ultimately, all conditioning is dysfunctional and even pathological because the conditions change and the responses become inappropriate," I continued.
"So even as a short-term solution, conditioning creates long-term problems," the old capitalist reasoned.
"That's right. Take for example our conditioned sexist and racist responses."
"Now most of the personnel being hired in the next decade are going to be from the ranks of women and minorities."
"We all have to learn to think systematically and productively," I said.
The old capitalist paused and then responded. *"The educational intervention creates the only leveraged and lasting value—thinking people capable of producing operational ideas."*
"The life of thinking feeds upon itself!"

PRIMING THE NEW CAPITALIZING SYSTEM

The old capitalist summarized the educational source of thinking:

"It seems to me that education becomes the thinking skills center. It not only empowers people to think productively. It also sets the model for thinking for the entire organization. By empowering through instruction in processing skills, instructors educate themselves out of their jobs. This empowering process creates the model for people to educate themselves out of their jobs and move on to bigger and better jobs."

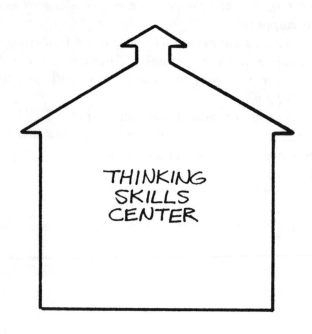

THE THINKING SKILLS CENTER

5. The Marketing Source of Profitability

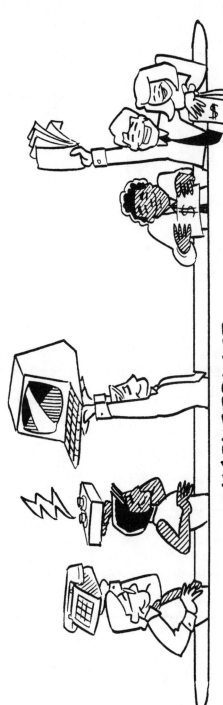

We landed at Edmonton, Gateway to the North, once a Hudson Bay Company fur-trading center and before that the home of Blackfeet and Cree Indians. We shared a taxi to our respective destinations, mine to conduct a seminar, his to find his roots and renew old associations.

"You know, I remember Edmonton when it was a one-horse town, little more than the fur-trading and mining supply center upon which it was built," the old capitalist began.

"It's quite a complete marketplace now."

"It just grew and grew!" the old capitalist exclaimed.

"Not quite," I remarked. *"It grew because it met people's needs. Maybe because it anticipated their needs."*

"It's the same in any business."

"Exactly. Those businesses grow that best meet and anticipate the consumers' needs."

"So it's not even a matter of meeting their needs. It's a matter of educating them to their future needs while simultaneously fulfilling those needs."

"It's a matter of creating a thinking relationship with the consumers," I emphasized.

"You know," said the old capitalist, *"I'm elated because I'm finally putting this picture of the New Capitalism together."*

CREATING A THINKING RELATIONSHIP

"Clearly, the source of profitability is the marketplace," he continued. *"Without a consumer, there can be no profit."*
"Because the conditions of the market are changing so rapidly, the only source of constancy is the marketing relationship between producer and consumer," I interjected.
"Even the producer and consumer are changing."
"They can use their changing relationship to each other's benefit—"
"By forming a deep and intense relationship based upon concern for each other's welfare!" the old capitalist offered.
"Like husband and wife, they can change to meet each other's as well as their own changing needs," I said. *"The secret to the marketing relationship is in growing."*
"The partners grow as the relationship grows," the old capitalist concluded.

SOURCES OF PROFITABILITY

We defined the profitable marketing system in terms of the marketing relationship. Productive producers and consumers relate to develop and deliver products and services that are tailored to meet consumer needs and, at the same time, are economical for consumer resources.

"So the marketing relationship that responds to consumer needs and resources is the key to financial profit," the old capitalist reflected.

"And the key to that relationship is the productivity of the producers and consumers," I added.

"Which is based upon their level of human and information capital development."

THE PROFITABLE MARKETING SYSTEM

We concluded that the productive consumer organization involved precisely the same dimensions.

"We used to say, 'What's good for the goose is good for the gander,'" the old capitalist mused.

"It's important to understand that in a full relationship, we are each concerned with the other's thinking sources of performance," I reminded him.

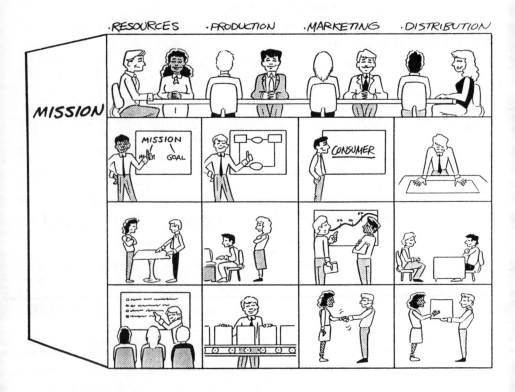

THE PRODUCTIVE CONSUMER ORGANIZATION

We had already defined the productive organization in terms of strategic operations, performance, and processing.
"It seems to me that thinking is the source of performance and performance is the source of the productivity of the processing operations," the old capitalist reviewed.

PROCESSING COMPONENTS

THE PRODUCTIVE ORGANIZATION

We pictured how that mutual concern translates itself in the marketing relationship.

"Both producer and consumer are committed to the other's productivity in all areas and levels of operations," I said.

"That's a profound commitment," the old capitalist noted. *"That's a growth commitment!"*

"Each will grow as the other grows."

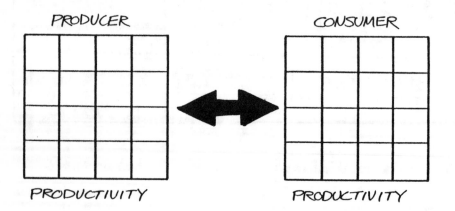

THE PROFITABLE MARKETING RELATIONSHIP

We translated the processing operations of a productive organization into the notion of a thinking environment.

"What we are really doing is creating a productive thinking environment," I said.

"People who think, relate and plan together grow together!" the old capitalist interjected.

"Creating a productive thinking environment implies a deep commitment to change."

"My job, then, is to create new work and eliminate old jobs."

"Above all, to grow," I reminded him.

"Not necessarily quantitative growth, but certainly qualitative growth," the old capitalist conjectured.

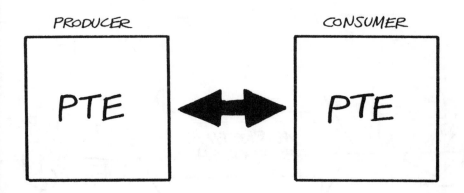

THE THINKING ENVIRONMENT

The thinking environment was extended to the thinking market.

"The producer's mission is to facilitate the development of the thinking environment for the consumer," I proposed.

"The producer helps the consumers to become productive and profitable by empowering them in thinking—independently, interpersonally, and interdependently," the old capitalist reflected.

"And the producer elicits a reciprocal commitment from the consumer."

"The consumer helps the producer to become productive and profitable by thinking interdependently."

"Yes, the key term is interdependence. We are each dependent upon the other for our growth."

"So the marketing relationship is defined by the thinking partnership," the old capitalist concluded.

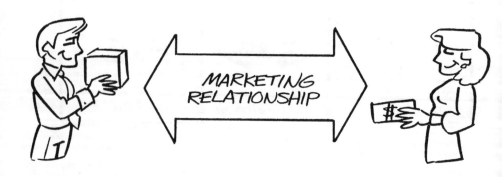

THE MARKETING RELATIONSHIP

"Marketing, then, is not the exchange of goods for dollars but rather the mutual processing of information concerning each other's needs and resources," the old capitalist continued.

"That's right. Because of the changing conditions of the market, we enter this intimate relationship with our consumers."

"We can relate to meet each other's needs."

"And we can relate to exceed each other's needs," I added.

With a puzzled look on his face, the old capitalist asked, *"You mean that we can create our own marketing conditions?"*

"Yes!" I emphatically answered. *"By defining a marketing relationship that is responsive, we can create market conditions that are initiative."*

"You mean that we can make things happen instead of waiting for them to happen?" the old capitalist continued.

"That is the human mission!"

"And the thinking relationship is the vehicle to the accomplishment of the human mission," the old capitalist added with a grin.

THE THINKING RELATIONSHIP

The old capitalist summarized the marketing source of profitability:

"If the heart of marketing is the marketing relationship, then the goal of marketing is to create a thinking market. A thinking market is one in which all parties—producers and consumers—think productively about their own as well as others' goals, needs, and resources. A thinking market is defined by the thinking relationship. It's one in which the marketing relationship literally 'thinks' about the parties to the relationship."

THE THINKING MARKET

THE THINKING MARKET

6. The New Capitalizing System

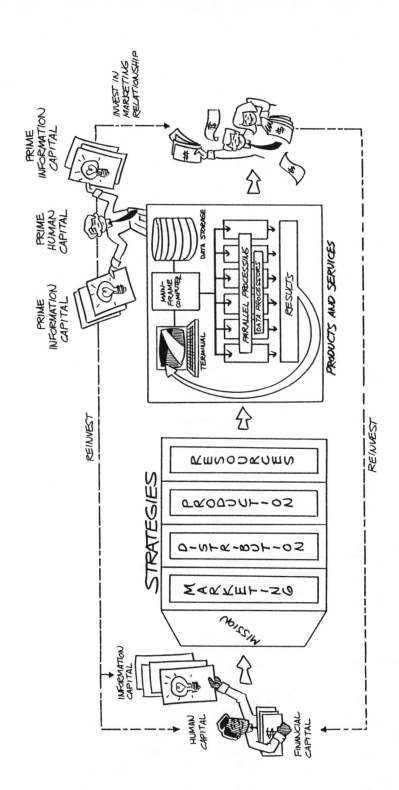

We lingered upon parting. We had become a part of each other's experience. We had defined an interdependent, thinking relationship by shared teaching and learning.

"We are in a period of transition between the financial-capital-based and the human- and information-capital-based views of economics," I said.

"I know. You can see it clearly when we funnel our creativity into the financing that has yielded a crescendo of corporate acquisitions, restructuring, and downsizing," the old capitalist added.

"These efforts yield no new ideas for creating wealth."

"They only mark the decline of financial capitalism's contributions to economic growth."

"Ahead lies a whole new era of human-and information-based capitalism."

"The Age of the New Capitalism!"

"Yes, one that contributes to—indeed creates—its own civilization."

THE AGE OF THE NEW CAPITALISM

"The real differences between the old and new capitalism are the capital ingredients," the old capitalist added.
"The capital ingredients impact every aspect of the capitalizing system: the mission, strategic goals, resource inputs, processing operations, results outputs, and marketing operations."
"So the New Capitalism is really an entirely new social system."
"That's right," I responded. *"The New Capitalism capitalizes upon the prepotent sources of economic impact—human and information capital—and accomplishes exponentially greater growth in productivity and profitability."*
"The New Capitalism capitalizes upon the most powerful forces in the universe—people and their ideas," the old capitalist concluded.

THE NEW CAPITALIZING SYSTEM

We discussed how the new capitalism begins with an expanded mission.

"The new capitalizing mission incorporates both producer and consumer targets and productivity as well as profitability benefit goals."

"It looks like you want the same things for the consumer that you want for the producer—productivity and profitability," the old capitalist interpreted.

"Exactly. The new mission is to impact consumer as well as producer productivity and profitability."

"I can see how you want the consumers to be productive and profitable in order to buy your products."

"Right," I said. *"Every cell impacts every other cell in the new mission. For example, producers need to become productive before they can help the consumers to become productive, which, in turn, leads to consumer profitability and, thus, producer profitability."*

"This is a mission that everyone—all levels of producers and consumers—can buy into. This is a shared value system."

	TARGETS	
GOALS	○CONSUMERS	○PRODUCERS
○PRODUCTIVITY	CONSUMER PRODUCTIVITY	PRODUCER PRODUCTIVITY
○PROFITABILITY	CONSUMER PROFITABILITY	PRODUCER PROFITABILITY

THE NEW CAPITALIZING MISSION

We continued our discussion of new strategic goals.

"So what happens to the consumers directly impacts what happens to the producers and vice versa," the old capitalist reflected.

"The new capital ingredients come into play in the form of the strategic goals," I responded. *"For example, the development and interaction of human and information capital is the basis for consumer as well as producer productivity."*

"This means that we have to help the consumers to develop human processing ingredients as well as to develop our own."

"Likewise we have to help the consumers to be profitable as well as ourselves," I added.

"So our business is to keep our consumers in business."

GOALS	TARGETS	
	∘CONSUMER	∘PRODUCER
∘PRODUCTIVITY	HC ⟷ IC	HC ⟷ IC
∘PROFITABILITY	$	$

THE NEW STRATEGIC GOALS

We extended our discussion to strategies accomplishing the mission.

"Our concern for consumer as well as producer benefits dictates that our strategies begin with marketing," I offered.

"In other words, we need to know the consumer's needs and resources if we are going to (1) impact the consumer's productivity and profitability, and (2) develop our own productivity and profitability."

"Yes, and we need to strategize about things like distribution or fulfilling and servicing consumer needs before producing the products."

"So mature new capitalistic corporations are market driven to accomplish productivity and profitability benefits for both consumers and producers," the old capitalist summarized.

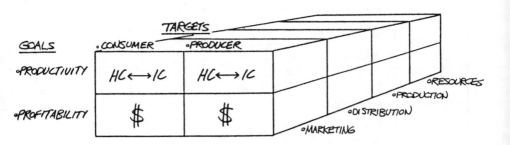

THE NEW STRATEGIES

We went on to discuss the processing operations of the new capitalizing system.

"The real sources of performance are the individual, unit, and organizational performances that occur within the processing operations."

"And the source of their power is processing," the old capitalist interpreted.

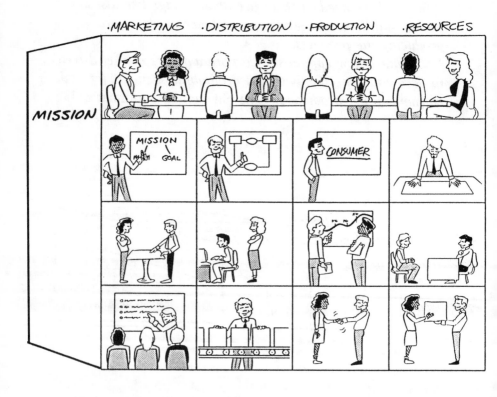

THE NEW CAPITALIZING OPERATIONS

"Each of the sources of performance has individual, inter-personal, and organizational sources of processing," I continued.

"So whether I'm seen at an individual work station or as part of a unit or even the entire organization, the source of my performance is thinking, relating, and planning," the old capitalist reflected.

"Processing is the source of performance that, in turn, yields productivity and profitability."

After a moment, the old capitalist concluded, *"Therefore, processing is the source of everything, and the new capital ingredients are the source of processing."*

PROCESSING COMPONENT

| ·INDIVIDUAL PERFORMANCE | ·UNIT PRODUCTION | ·ORGANIZATION PRODUCTIVITY |

THE NEW PROCESSING OPERATIONS

110

The discussion focused upon the capital inputs to the new capitalizing system.

"Since human and information capital account for most of economic productivity growth, then the new capital inputs must emphasize these ingredients."

"This means recruiting and training for thinking," the old capitalist interpreted.

"Financial resource inputs must also be invested as catalytic agents for the processing."

"This means purchasing the materials, equipment, and other things we need to produce our products and deliver our services," the old capitalist added.

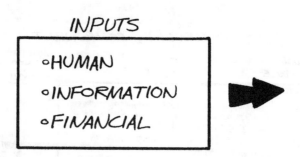

INPUTS

∘HUMAN

∘INFORMATION

∘FINANCIAL

THE NEW CAPITAL RESOURCE INPUTS

The discussion extended to the new capital outputs.
"Obviously, the new capital outputs emphasize new human and information capital along with improved products and services," the old capitalist began.
"And these new capital outputs may be more valuable in the long run than the products and services."
"That's because they're the source of new ideas about producing and marketing new products and services."
"Right," I said nodding my head. *"And whereas the products and services are a source of current benefits, the new capital ingredients are the source of future benefits."*

CAPITAL OUTPUTS

- HUMAN CAPITAL'
- INFORMATION CAPITAL'
- PRODUCTS AND SERVICES

THE NEW CAPITAL OUTPUTS

The discussion emphasized the marketing relationship as the core of the New Capitalism.

"The marketing relationship is both the means and the ends of the New Capitalism."

"Instead of manipulating people to buy our goods, we relate to them to meet both of our needs," the old capitalist interjected.

"It is important to emphasize that in a fully productive and profitable relationship, every cell of the producer's operations relates to every cell of the consumer operations."

"So the marketing relationship is the source of creating new business as well as fulfilling old business for both producer and consumer," the old capitalist concluded.

THE NEW CAPITAL MARKETING RELATIONSHIP

The old capitalist reviewed new capital accumulation and reinvestment:

"I can see how the new capitalizing system is reinvigorated with new doses of capital ingredients. The people are smarter. The ideas are better. The business is richer because of success in the marketplace. We need only to reinvest these new capital ingredients in the next cycle of capitalizing to become even more smart, operational, and rich."

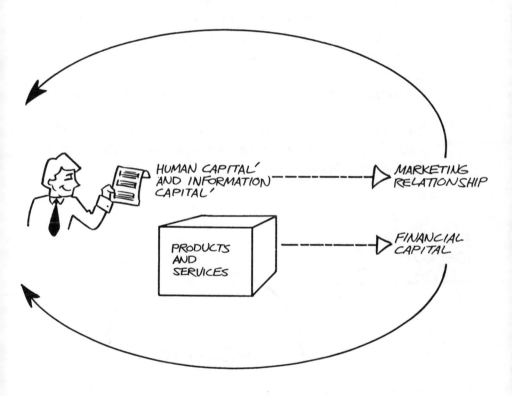

**THE NEW CAPITAL ACCUMULATION
AND REINVESTMENT**

"I now understand why we could no longer predict economic success using the old capitalist system," the old capitalist said gleefully. *"We just couldn't account for more than 15 percent of economic growth no matter how much we analyzed the conditions of financial capital."*

"Right. You weren't analyzing the relevant sources of growth," I answered.

"And I also understand why all of the financial strategies—downsizing, restructuring, and the like—are doomed to fail," the old capitalist continued. *"The strategists eliminate the best talent because this talent finds irrational treatment intolerable. And they take with them the most valuable information capital—their ideas about the projects they have been working on."*

I showed him how the growth curve follows the new capital ingredients curve.

The old capitalist remarked, *"So for short-term profits the financial strategies precipitate long-term losses based upon their elimination of the new capital ingredients."*

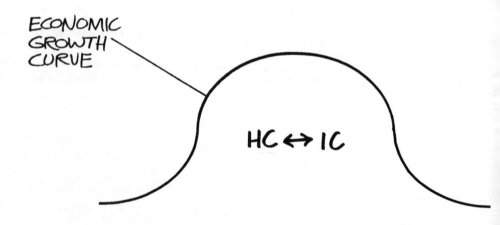

ECONOMIC
GROWTH
CURVE

HC ↔ IC

SHORT-TERM PROFITS AND LONG-TERM LOSSES

"In a healthy system the talent is empowered by thinking skills to become the source of future growth," I said.
"So the growth curve reflects the new capital ingredients at work," the old capitalist responded.
"Yes, short-term investments in human and information capital have long-term payoffs in financial benefits."
"It all boils down to a question of trust, then. The real talent simply will not trust the corporation and they are the corporation's most valuable asset."
"And the question of trust cuts both ways: the employees must trust the corporation if they think themselves out of their jobs, and the corporation must trust the employees to invest their efforts in the corporation, which has invested in teaching them to think."
"So the fundamental assumption of the New Capitalism is trust," the old capitalist concluded.
"We truly are interdependent partners—both as producers and in our relations to consumers."
"Ultimately, that extends to all of our trading partners," the old capitalist added.
"Yes, we cooperate with each other in order to compete to service our consumers."

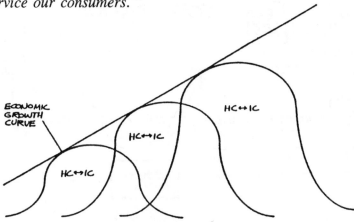

SHORT-TERM INVESTMENTS AND LONG-TERM BENEFITS

The old capitalist summarized the new capitalizing vehicle in vivid imagery:

"I think of the new capitalizing system like a modern truck bound to accomplish the marketing mission. The key elements are the human and information capital, which guide the vehicle and the resources that provide the rear-wheel drive to support the front-wheel drive of marketing. The truck continues to be fueled but not dominated by financial capital. It's a modern vehicle appropriate to the Information Age. It gets us where we want to go with maximum effectiveness and efficiency. It leaves us and everyone else involved better off than it found us—better off financially, better off operationally, better off as human beings. It dwarfs the contributions of the old capitalizing vehicle."

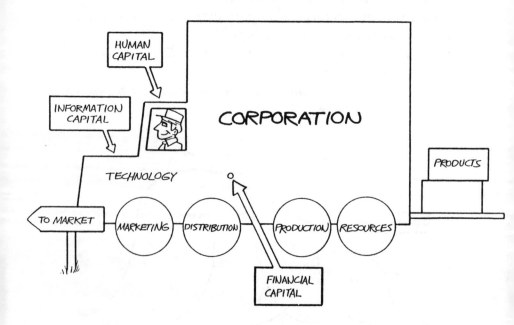

THE NEW CAPITALIZING VEHICLE

III. SUMMARY AND CONCLUSIONS

7. The Thinking Theory of Value

The Utilitarian Theory of Values

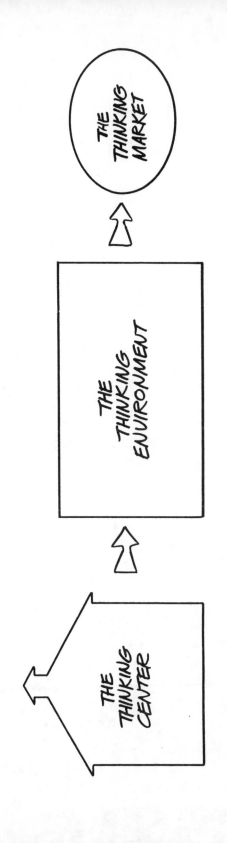

I invited the old capitalist to join me the next day in my seminar with youthful leaders from the private and public sectors. He obliged, and confidently introduced our audience to the conclusions of our extended conversation on the Age of the New Capitalism:

"The Age of the New Capitalism really has three critical processes in which human and information capital inputs are formed and related. The first one is the lifelong and continuous education and training process. The second one is the constantly improving processing operations that produce the products and services along with improved human and information capital. The third one is the continuously growing marketing relationship between producer and consumer that yields for both of them not only financial capital but prime human and information capital. Together these processes define the thinking theory of value."

THE THINKING THEORY OF VALUE

Together we reviewed for the audience our conclusions concerning education as the source of thinking: human and information resources are developed into the human and information capital that define the ingredients of human processing.

"Education should empower people to engineer their own human condition," I offered.

"But as currently practiced, it merely regurgitates useless facts and concepts," the old capitalist interjected.

"It is because the learners are unable to process changing knowledge that both learners and knowledge are useless."

"So the mission of education is to teach thinking skills."

"To do this, education has to be completely redesigned to become the supplier of the capital inputs that are invested in the capitalizing process."

"Education has to get down to business!" one of the participants suggested.

"Or get into business!" another complemented.

EDUCATION—THE EMPOWERING SOURCE

We continued to discuss the human and information capital inputs as the energizing ingredients of the New Capitalism.

"The differences in inputs are what make differences in outputs," I said. *"Since the new capital resources of human processing account for most of economic productivity growth, then we must emphasize these resources on input. Since education accounts for most of human processing, then we must prepare these new capital resources systematically."*

"So education yields thinking, and thinking yields productivity growth," the old capitalist added.

"The New Capitalism begins with the new capital investments," one of the members of the audience reflected.

"We are the New Capitalists!" others echoed.

INVESTING CAPITAL—THE ENERGIZING INGREDIENTS

Our discussion emphasized human processing as the capitalizing processes in which these resource inputs are capitalized upon.

"Again, human processing involves the synergistic relationship of human and information capital."

"I think of it as the growing process," the old capitalist offered. *"We grow people and information as well as products and sources. We grow them by thinking, relating, and planning."*

"Capitalizing is growing!" one of the New Capitalists offered.

HUMAN PROCESSING—THE CAPITALIZING PROCESSES

What the audience found so exciting theoretically was the potential of processing.

"The heart of processing is in expanding and narrowing," I offered. *"First, we expand the options to our current systems. Then we use our values to narrow the options to productive systems."*

"It creates enormous potential," the old capitalist suggested.

"Potentially, our options may be expanded infinitely."

"So our alternatives are limitless."

"Similarly, our values may be expanded or elevated infinitely."

"So our values are also limitless."

"It is when we expand our options to the point where we have satisfied our elevated values that we begin to increase our potential performance."

"It is just like we have been discussing—expanding the options and elevating the values of the New Capitalism," the old capitalist elaborated.

"So ultimately, our potential is infinite," the New Capitalists universally concluded.

THE INFINITE POSSIBILITIES

"It is these infinite possibilities that define human freedom," I continued.

"So by expanding my options and values, I am expanding my degrees of freedom," the old capitalist reflected.

"We're really elevating our options and values to find better ways of doing things."

"There's always a better way."

"We're restricted only by our conditioning."

"So freedom is the absence of conditioning."

"Or put more positively, freedom is the presence of processing."

"My freedom is a function of my thinking skills."

"In a free society, we have the opportunity to exercise the freedom to think creatively. Conversely, in a totalitarian society, we are conditioned to think the leader's way or the central committee's way."

"We may define our freedom not only in terms of the absence of restrictions but also in terms of the presence of thinking," the New Capitalists voiced.

"And ultimately, the battle within corporations as well as within world society is between freedom and totalitarianism—between thinking and conditioning."

"The ultimate battle is whether the world will be free or unfree, and that depends upon whether we learn to think productively," the New Capitalists summarized.

HUMAN FREEDOM

We recognized this potential in improved human performance.

"When we measure human performance, we measure not only the responses performed but also the products and services produced."

"This is more or less the bureaucratic level of feedback that tells us what we did and how well we did it," the old capitalist interpreted.

"We can offer this feedback to the personnel themselves to manage the improvement in their own performance."

"So measuring human performance is really a form of information capital that can be used to improve performance by self-supervision," the New Capitalists agreed.

RESPONSES   PRODUCTS   SERVICES

HUMAN PERFORMANCE

Still more important is the feedback of our human productivity outcomes.

"Human productivity simply compares our results outputs with our resource inputs—our results effectiveness with our resource efficiency."

"So if human processing accounts for almost all of productivity growth, then we should be improving our results outputs while reducing our resource inputs," the old capitalist interjected.

"Ultimately, our mission is to approach infinite outputs by investing infinitesimal inputs, like Jack Kilby, making the enormously powerful microchip out of one of our cheapest elements, sand or silicon," one of the New Capitalists suggested.

HUMAN PRODUCTIVITY

I could see that some members of the audience were
confused.

*"You feel confused because this seems so abstract and you
can't quite concretize it,"* I responded.

*"We're trying to figure out how infinite productivity is
possible,"* they explained.

"Think about the sources of human productivity," the old
capitalist directed.

*"Human and information capital invested in human
processing?"* they asked.

*"Exactly. When we maximize our human and information
capital inputs, we minimize all other resource inputs,"* the
old capitalist interpreted.

*"So if we invest actualized thinkers and the universe of in-
formation, we may not need to invest any other resources
in producing exponentially better results,"* the New
Capitalists summarized.

*"We may, for example, adapt an already existing system
and, by adding our own modifications, multiply our productivity many times over."*

*"We don't always have to reinvent the wheel but we do
have to process its system productively,"* one New Capitalist offered.

"In our own ways we really can become Kilbys," the Kil-
bian concluded.

KILBIAN PRODUCTIVITY

Even the ultimate old capitalistic test of feedback—the bottom line—is met in exciting new ways in the marketplace.

"Human profitability simply means that people have benefited from the effort. Not only did the products meet the financial tests of the marketplace but also the productivity and profitability tests of the consumer."

"It's what we call a win-win situation," the old capitalist inserted.

"Both consumers and producers are served by the marketing relationship."

"So human profitability is determined by the marketing relationship," one New Capitalist summarized.

"And ultimately that relationship has infinite potential," all seemed to agree.

HUMAN PROFITABILITY

The ultimate new capitalistic test of actualizing human and information potential is also met in exciting new ways in and out of the marketplace.

"Perhaps the greatest benefit of the thinking theory of value is found in the development of new levels of human and information capital."

"They may be very valuable byproducts," the old capitalist reflected.

"In the end, they may be more valuable outputs than the products and services in the marketplace. Whereas the products' value remains relatively constant, the value of human and information capital is growing exponentially."

"But people and information are not treated like multi-million dollar properties!" a chorus of New Capitalist voices protested.

"That is the problem of their managers and not of the people and information, for their value is huge," the old capitalist replied.

HUMAN AND INFORMATION POTENTIAL

Above all else, the thinking theory of value is an ethical system.

"The thinking theory of value emphasizes human processing for human purposes."

"I've always felt so torn because I was fragmented by ethical and economic motives," the old capitalist interjected.

"That's just the point. Economic and human goals are served by the same capitalizing system."

"What is economics if not the area of application of psychology?" the old capitalist asked and then answered with another question, *"What is psychology if not the thinking source of economic relationships?"*

"Psychology and economics are integrated in a unifying thinking theory of value."

"I'm so excited because I feel like I've been put back together again!" the old capitalist concluded.

"We feel hope for our future as capitalists," one of the New Capitalists said.

"Rather than shame for our past and disappointment in our present!" another added.

THE HUMAN ETHIC

We concluded with the recycling of the thinking process.
"Of course, in productive and profitable corporations, the thinking process is recycled by reinvesting human and information capital as well as financial capital."
"Just like a healthy human recycles feedback, a productive organization recycles its new capital," the old capitalist suggested.
"The lifeline of the corporation is this investment of new capital."
"It's probably more like spiraling than recycling. The spirals get bigger and bigger as we get better and better," one of the New Capitalists suggested to audience approval.

RECYCLING THE THINKING PROCESS

"There is nothing inherently true in the nature of our current capitalistic system other than that it is a system for dealing with what is most important."

"It was designed by human choice, not Godly voice," the old capitalist added.

"It is for each generation to choose its own economic destiny."

"And its system for fulfilling that destiny."

"The thinking theory of value simply empowers people to engineer their own system."

"The capitalizing system is merely what is most important in the system of their choice."

"So we can become masters of our universes—"

"As well as ourselves!"

"We can create and meet human values," one of the New Capitalists offered.

"Thinking is the basic human value!" another concluded.

THE VALUE THEORY OF THINKING

The old capitalist summarized his understanding of the implications of the thinking theory of value for the Age of the New Capitalism:

"Perhaps most important, we can define the operations of the thinking processes involved in the thinking universe: the human and information resource development processes (HRD ↔ IRD), which produce capital value; the human and informaton capitalizing processes (HC ↔ IC), which produce new capital value; the marketing processes of producer and consumer capitalizing (PC ↔ CC), which add still greater capital value. It is this technology that enables real human change. Defining the processing operations means that we can achieve them. Human goals are limited only by our thinking skills. Indeed, human goals are defined by our thinking skills and, in their processing, define our humanity."

"We are hopeful because there is a better way that includes—indeed, requires—all of our potential," the New Capitalists concluded.

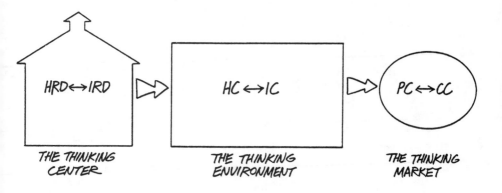

THE THINKING INGREDIENTS OF THE NEW CAPITALISM

EPILOGUE:
PREPARING FOR THE AGE OF
THE NEW CAPITALISM

THE ADVANCEMENT OF CIVILIZATION

ERAS	SOCIAL & POLITICAL	SCIENCE & TECHNOLOGY	ECONOMICS & COMMERCE	CURRENCY OF EXCHANGE	COMMUNICATION	EDUCATION
PREHISTORIC	FAMILIES & TRIBES	CONTROL OF FIRE	FINITE RESOURCES	BARTER	ORAL	SPIRITUAL INDUCTION
AGRARIAN	TOWNS & CITIES	CULTIVATION & DOMESTICATION	LAND SOURCE OF VALUE	BARTER & SYMBOLS	PRINT	SPIRITUAL & APPRENTICE
INDUSTRIAL	NATION—STATES	MECHANICAL PROCESSING	FINANCIAL CAPITAL	MONETARY (GOLD STANDARD)	TELEPHONIC	SCIENTIFIC (BASIC SKILLS)
ELECTRONIC	INTERNATIONAL ALLIANCES	COMPUTER PROCESSING	HUMAN & INFORMATION RESOURCES	MONETARY	COMPUTER	TECHNICAL SKILLS
INFORMATION	GLOBAL VILLAGE	HUMAN PROCESSING	HUMAN & INFORMATION CAPITAL	INFORMATION	TELECOM-MUNICATION	LEARNING SKILLS
IDEATION	CULTURAL MARKETPLACE PROCESSING	HIGHER-ORDER	THINKING CAPITAL	IDEAS	NETWORKING	THINKING SKILLS

On the flight back from Edmonton, I was coming down from my high. With the old capitalist I had had a chance to explore and understand the most important human issue of our time, the entry into the Age of the New Capitalism. The trip there was like going up the emotional keyboard: from cynicism and disappointment to interest, conviction, and commitment, to elation, even ecstasy, and confidence, confidence in the future of humankind. The flight back was like a trip down the emotional keyboard: from the high of ecstasy and confidence to the low of doubts, bordering on cynicism once again. The crucial question was this: Even in the face of our understanding of the implications of choices between the old capitalism and the New Capitalism, were we capable of making the choice? The implications are profound for us as individuals, communities, nations, and peoples on this planet Earth.

THE PROFOUND CHOICE

In this context, I remembered the gist of our conversation concerning the old capitalist's readiness for change:

"I believe that change will always be with us," he said. *"That is part of the human condition that God placed upon us. But we are also blessed with the spirit of inquiry that allows us to question our conditions. And we were given a brain that allows us to learn to adapt to our condition or even change our condition."*

"It's this spirit of inquiry that interests me," I interjected. *"That's the spirit that is passed on from generation to generation. Driven by love of others, search for truth, enjoyment of beauty, drive for excellence, the individual human spirit probes the unknown to make it knowable, even to alter it."*

"How exciting it is to discover this spirit in oneself!"

THE DOMINANCE OF THE HUMAN SPIRIT

"So the human spirit is as constant as the change around us," I continued.

"Yes, the human spirit is what links generations and civilizations through the social, scientific, economic, and educational contributions about which you have taught me," the old capitalist replied.

"We have taught each other."

"And that teaching and learning is what made it all possible. I want to thank you for being my teacher on this trip."

"I want to thank you for helping me with the next generation."

"That's it!" the old capitalist concluded. *"Teaching and learning and respecting and loving—those are the sources of the human spirit."*

"And when two of these spirits touch, as we have, generations and civilizations link."

TEACHING, LEARNING, AND LOVING

During the entire flight, I reflected upon the old capitalist's enthusiasm for information and eagerness for learning. I remembered our final exchange:

"For me, new information is new opportunity, and thinking about it is taking advantage of the opportunity," the old capitalist began.

"It's like being born anew with each new piece of information."

"Information is an opportunity to grow."

"And it doesn't matter how old you are chronologically."

"I can grow forever."

"We can die growing."

"As long as this old brain keeps working, it's not too late for me."

"That's exactly why your brain keeps working," I exclaimed.

"And it's not too early for others," the old capitalist concluded.

NOT TOO EARLY

I remember the last question the old capitalist had asked: *"What lies ahead?"*
"The natural extension or culmination of the Information Age is an Age of Ideation."
"An age in which ideas dominate?" the old capitalist questioned.
"Yes, whereas the source of economic analysis is global, the source of economic impact is individual."
"The source of economic growth is in the ideas of the individual."
"Ideas undergird all exchange in the marketplace."
"In other words, ideas are really the currency of exchange," the old capitalist added.
"As well as the currency of change!" I added.
"The thinking human is the source of all value."
"The thinking human is the basic value."
"It sounds like we're defining our humanity by the use of our intellects," the old capitalist said.
"Or defining our intellects by our commitment to our humanity," I added.

THE AGE OF IDEATION

"So capitalism is really only a theory of the changing conditions of wealth, however we choose to define it," the old capitalist reflected.

"And capitalism may create these conditions as well as respond to them."

"It's simple for me. If capitalism is in tune with changing conditions—as you say, synergistic with change—it is an enormously productive vehicle for emphasizing what is important for advancing civilization."

"And if it is not in tune with changing conditions?" I asked.

"Then it is worse than useless. It is retarding or even destructive for people and relations between them."

"The secret of capitalism is that it recreates itself," I shared.

"So by increasing the range of ideas it increases the odds of exceeding the changing requirements," the old capitalist interpreted.

"Capitalism is people!"

THE NEW AND CHANGING CAPITALISM

I hardly noticed passing through the sparkling spread of Toronto and the jammed lightening bug jar of New York on my way home. This time I sat by the window, my gaze unfocused, my mind lost in contemplating a darkness about to descend upon the civilization we have known. Unless. Unless we empower each other to redefine economic relations and human existence. I recalled the last words which the old capitalist had directed at me:

"Capitalism is really a theory of change. It adapts to and causes the changing eras of humanity. I hope I live long enough to experience the next era."

In landing, I saw that man's blinking lights once again pierce the darkness.

LOOKING FORWARD